T0401414

US ARMY

BY CYNTHIA KENNEDY HENZEL

CONTENT CONSULTANT

J. Paul Pope
Professor of Practice
Lyndon B. Johnson School of Public Affairs
University of Texas at Austin
Senior Fellow
Intelligence Studies Project

Essential Library

An Imprint of Abdo Publishing | abdobooks.com

ABDOBOOKS.COM

Published by Abdo Publishing, a division of ABDO, PO Box 398166, Minneapolis, Minnesota 55439. Copyright © 2021 by Abdo Consulting Group, Inc. International copyrights reserved in all countries. No part of this book may be reproduced in any form without written permission from the publisher. Essential Library™ is a trademark and logo of Abdo Publishing.

Printed in the United States of America, North Mankato, Minnesota.
042020
092020

THIS BOOK CONTAINS RECYCLED MATERIALS

Cover Photo: Staff Sgt. Justin P. Morelli/US Army/Defense Visual Information Distribution Service
Interior Photos: Cpl. Alisha Grezlik/Defense Visual Information Distribution Service, 4–5; Staff Sgt. Tina Villalobos/US Army/Defense Visual Information Distribution Service, 8; Steven A. Davis/US Navy/Defense Visual Information Distribution Service, 11; North Wind Picture Archives, 14–15, 18; AP Images, 23; Jim Collins/AP Images, 25; Mark C. Olsen/US Army National Guard/Defense Visual Information Distribution Service, 26; Senior Airman Codie Trimble/US Air Force/Defense Visual Information Distribution Service, 28–29; Kenneth Drylie/IMCOM/US Army, 31; Spc. Jarvis Mace/US Army National Guard/Defense Visual Information Distribution Service, 32; T. Whitney/Shutterstock Images, 37; Scott T. Sturkol/US Army/Defense Visual Information Distribution Service, 39, 62–63, 64; Staff Sgt. Stacy L. Pearsall/US Air Force, 42; 1st Lt. Ryan DeBooy/US Army/Defense Visual Information Distribution Service, 44–45; Maya Alleruzzo/AP Images, 47; Sgt. 1st Class John Etheridge/US Army/Defense Visual Information Distribution Service, 50; Pfc. Christopher McKenna/Defense Visual Information Distribution Service, 54–55; Spc. Sean Harding/US Army Reserve/Defense Visual Information Distribution Service, 59; Sgt. 1st Class Scott Raymond/US Army National Guard/Defense Visual Information Distribution Service, 68; Staff Sgt. Shejal Pulivarti/US Army Africa/Defense Visual Information Distribution Service, 72–73; Staff Sgt. David Chapman/Defense Visual Information Distribution Service, 76; Capt. Charles An/US Army/Defense Visual Information Distribution Service, 79; Spc. Stephanie Homan/US Army/Defense Visual Information Distribution Service, 82–83; Spc. Shardesia Washington/US Army/Defense Visual Information Distribution Service, 85; Staff Sgt. Lorne W. Neff/120th PAD/JTF–GTMO Public Affairs/Alamy, 89; Spc. Jeffery Sandstrum/US Army, 90; Sgt. 1st Class Gregory Williams/Massachusetts National Guard/Defense Visual Information Distribution Service, 92–93; Sgt. 1st Class Gary A. Witte/US Army/Defense Visual Information Distribution Service, 97

Editor: Charly Haley
Series Designer: Nikki Nordby

LIBRARY OF CONGRESS CONTROL NUMBER: 2019954353

PUBLISHER'S CATALOGING-IN-PUBLICATION DATA

Names: Henzel, Cynthia Kennedy, author.
Title: US Army / by Cynthia Kennedy Henzel
Description: Minneapolis, Minnesota : Abdo Publishing, 2021 | Series: US military careers | Includes online resources and index.
Identifiers: ISBN 9781532192272 (lib. bdg.) | ISBN 9781098210175 (ebook)
Subjects: LCSH: Armies--Juvenile literature. | Members of the Armed Forces--Juvenile literature. | Military power--Juvenile literature. | United States. Army--History--Juvenile literature. | Armed Forces--Juvenile literature.
Classification: DDC 355.12--dc23

CONTENTS

CHAPTER 1

CLEARING THE WAY

AUS Army combat engineer, responsible for clearing the road ahead for the infantry massing behind him, brought his assault breacher vehicle (ABV) to a halt. His commander, a lieutenant, manned the 12.7-mm machine gun mounted on top of the vehicle. Reconnaissance, or surveillance of enemy territory, showed that the insurgents had fled the day before, and the long, dusty road between the US Army soldiers and the

Army combat engineers train in assault breacher vehicles at the National Training Center in Fort Irwin, California.

village looked empty. But the combat engineer had no doubt they were about to enter a field of land mines and improvised explosive devices (IEDs). His team's job was to clear the way for the US infantry platoon behind them that would occupy the town. Whether it meant removing obstacles; building bridges, roads, and defenses; or, like today, filling in craters and clearing the road ahead of land mines and IEDs, the team of combat engineers was on the job.

MILITARY WORKING DOGS

Military working dogs are an important part of many army units. Each dog has a specialty. They are trained to find drugs, money, explosives such as IEDs, or anything else that their noses can detect. Dogs may help soldiers clear buildings and provide nonlethal protection, such as barking and taking down enemies without killing them. The military has about 2,700 dogs working in war zones. Between 2005 and 2010, US military working dogs in Afghanistan and Iraq found about 12,500 pounds (5,700 kg) of explosives, saving thousands of lives.[1] The job of military working dog handler is a highly trained army position that teaches soldiers to handle, care for, and train military working dogs.

"This is where we'll launch the first line charges," the lieutenant said, stepping toward the back of the ABV. Along with a mine sweep team and an IED dog, a group of vehicles—including two more ABVs and a Humvee vehicle—took defensive positions behind the lieutenant's ABV. The Humvee vehicle carried the TALON robot, a small unmanned vehicle used to protect soldiers against IEDs. The lieutenant raised one of the two rocket launchers on his ABV.

"Three-two-one. Fire in the hole. Fire in the hole. Fire in the hole!" he yelled.

The lieutenant then pushed the red toggle, and a string of explosives launched 460 feet (140 m) forward and landed on the road ahead. Boom! Fire shot up, smoke filled the air, and clods of dirt rained down. The soldiers cheered. "Just like the Fourth of July!" someone shouted.

The combat engineer hunched behind the safety of the ABV's steel plating. As the smoke lifted, he inched the vehicle forward. A hundred meters at a time, his team cleared the road leading toward the village ahead. Soldiers acting as lookouts searched for snipers, their eyes sweeping the rooftops.

As the team got closer to the houses, the lieutenant ordered the plow on the ABV to be lowered. This attachment would snag any trip lines attached to IEDs.

"I've caught one!" yelled the combat engineer.

"Back up, slowly," ordered the lieutenant.

The ABV backed up until the team could see a wire that the plow had pulled from the dusty road. There was no doubt that the wire was attached to a deadly number of explosives.

"Bring up the TALON," called the lieutenant.

SAPPERS

Military combat engineers are sometimes called *sappers*. The name comes from the 1600s, when soldiers dug covered trenches to attack forts and then dug under the fort walls to collapse them. The tunnels were called *saps*, and the diggers became known as sappers. Today's sappers are frontline soldiers who clear the way. They not only build bridges and roads but also clear obstacles; build weapon stands, airstrips, and helipads; and take care of whatever is needed to move the battle forward. The army offers its Sapper Leader Course to other US military branches too. It teaches leadership skills, advanced tactics, and how to work across military branches as a team. Military members who complete the rigorous 28-day course wear the sapper tab on their uniforms.

Soldiers use the TALON robot to safely locate and dispose of enemy ★ explosives. They use a remote control to operate the robot from a distance.

Two soldiers unloaded the 100-pound (45 kg) robot. A sergeant opened a small suitcase that contained the TALON's radio controls. The robot rolled on tracks like a tank as the sergeant steered it close to the IED and examined the ground with the robot's cameras.

"Looks like we can blow it here!" the sergeant called. She backed the robot away. Another soldier placed two small packs of explosives near the IED and then stepped away. Just then, a young boy peeked out of a door to a civilian house down the road.

"Get back!" yelled one of the soldiers, and the boy darted back inside.

"Three-two-one. Fire in the hole. Fire in the hole. Fire in the hole!" called the sergeant. Then she used the robot to set off the explosion. Boom! The IED was neutralized.

The lieutenant called in the minesweepers, and that unit entered the village to clear the main street. A dog trained to sniff out IEDs and its handler followed. Each time they found something, the TALON took care of it.

Hours later, the hot, dusty crew was done. The village was safe for the advancing infantry soldiers and the people who lived there.

ONE OF MANY

The US Army's mission is to protect and defend the United States with ground forces, armor, and weapons. It is expected to be able to deploy, fight, and win decisively against any enemy. Combat engineer is just one of more than 150 jobs the army needs to complete its mission.[2] Other combat soldiers include infantry, cavalry, and communications specialists. Soldiers in maintenance jobs keep equipment, including the TALON and a huge assortment of vehicles and weapons, in good condition.

VETERAN BENEFITS

Veterans are entitled to many benefits for their military service. Under the GI Bill, veterans can receive money from the government for college tuition or job training. They may qualify for low-cost home loans and low-cost health, auto, and life insurance. The army also helps veterans get civilian jobs once they leave the army. Veterans who have made their careers in the army get retirement benefits, too. Besides the benefits offered by the government, many private companies and corporations offer discounts to veterans for dining, entertainment, travel, and other services to show their appreciation for military service.

Health care through veterans' hospitals is one government benefit offered to veterans. This includes psychological care if needed. However, veterans' hospitals have had problems helping the large number of veterans who need their services. At the beginning of 2019, 70 percent of veterans' hospitals had wait times that were longer than at non-veterans' hospitals.[3] To address this problem, a new policy went into effect in early 2019 with the goal of helping veterans get health care at non-veterans' facilities when veterans' hospitals are not available in a timely manner.

★ A wide variety of interests, from computers to driving, can be applied to US Army careers.

They make necessary repairs, often on a tight timeline.

Support personnel make sure that soldiers in the field have the equipment they need, from ammunition to foot powder, and truck drivers deliver the supplies. Other soldiers are in charge of food, clothing, and health care.

Army soldiers in other specialties work from a distance to help support the commanders in the field. They analyze conditions on the ground using information gathered from drones, satellites, and GPS. They create the maps and images commanders need to make informed decisions. Some are linguists who help communicate with residents of foreign countries where US Army soldiers are working. Others are internet specialists.

Outside of combat zones, the army offers a large number of jobs that support the troops. Like any organization, the army has a payroll, insurance, and retirement and education benefits—someone must keep track of the soldiers, veterans, and their families to ensure they receive their pay and benefits. The army hires medical personnel, from nurses to dentists, to care for the troops. It also needs

TALKING TO A RECRUITER

US Army recruiters are available in every community in the country. They sometimes visit schools or appear at community events. People can find local recruiters by going to the official US Army website and searching by zip code or by looking up a recruiter in a telephone directory. Recruiters are the bridge between the army and those interested in army service or an army career. They are there to answer questions about what joining the army means. They also help people navigate the enlistment process. Recruiters can provide information about military jobs, training requirements, college tuition, and benefits, as well as answer other questions. People interested in joining the army can take a mini aptitude test to see whether they can qualify for enlistment and to learn what jobs might be available for them.

barbers, dietitians, musicians, and lawyers. Along with providing a host of career opportunities, the US Army offers training and advanced education.

RECRUITMENT

Every soldier who is recruited must be physically fit. Once they sign up, new recruits take an aptitude test. That test helps them choose from the many career opportunities to find jobs they are interested in and qualified for.

Army recruiters explain the opportunities and demands of army enlistment to new recruits. They answer questions about particular jobs in the army and questions about civilian jobs that might be available after military service. Army careers aim to provide skills and values such as organization, self-discipline, reliability, and commitment.

CHAPTER 2

THE HISTORY OF THE US ARMY

Army soldiers have been called upon to defend the nation both at home and overseas since before the United States became a country. The army was the country's first military branch. The Second Continental Congress formed the Continental army on June 14, 1775, so that the 13 American

George Washington led the United States'
first army, the Continental army.

colonies could wage war against the British. George Washington
was unanimously elected to head the army as a general
and commander in chief. Washington, who later became the
country's first president, led the Continental army to victory
against overwhelming British forces and won independence
for the colonies. In 1783, Washington thwarted a plan for a
military takeover of the government, setting a precedent for
civilian control of the military—meaning that civilian members
of the government, in addition to trained soldiers, can make
decisions about the military. That division of power between

the military and civilian government was enshrined in the US Constitution by making the president the commander in chief and giving Congress the sole power to declare war and control military spending.

In 1802, the first US military academy was established at West Point, New York, to train new military leaders for the fledgling country. In the first half of the 1800s, the army fought and won two international wars, the War of 1812 (1812–1815) against the British and the Mexican-American War (1846–1848).

BLACK SOLDIERS

During the American Revolutionary War (1775–1783), black and white soldiers served together in the US Army. But after the war, that integration ended. During the Civil War, black soldiers fought for the US Army in segregated units. One unit, Company C, 54th Massachusetts, showed extreme bravery while attempting to capture a Confederate fort. Sergeant William Carney of that unit was the first black soldier to receive the Medal of Honor, the nation's highest military award. Buffalo Soldiers, members of all-black US cavalry and infantry units from 1867 to 1896, protected white settlers in the West from Native Americans who were resisting being forced onto reservations. They later protected Native Americans from illegal encroachment by white settlers on Native American lands. Renowned for their discipline and courage, 14 Buffalo Soldiers received the Medal of Honor.[1] Black soldiers served in segregated units such as the Harlem Hellfighters in World War I (1914–1918) and the 761st Tank Battalion in World War II (1939–1945). In 1948, President Harry S. Truman signed Executive Order 9981, declaring that the US Army could not discriminate based on race, skin color, religion, or national origin. The final segregated army unit was disbanded in 1954.

During 1860 and 1861, 11 southern states seceded from the United States to form the Confederate States of America. This action led to the Civil War (1861–1865). About one-third of the US Army's officers left to join the Confederate army. In 1863, the US Army established its first draft for soldiers. The Confederacy had already instituted a draft for soldiers the year before. More than three million people served in the army during the Civil War. At the end of the war, more than one million volunteers remained in the army. However, most of these volunteers returned home by the following year. In 1866, Congress established a standing army of 54,000 soldiers.[2] Most of the army at this time served at forts in the American West. Soldiers helped force Native American tribes onto reservations.

THE ARMY REORGANIZES

The beginning of the Spanish-American War in 1898 required a rapid expansion of the US Army. Government and military leaders saw a need for an army that was more organized and had a trained reserve of soldiers. Secretary of War Elihu Root, serving under President William McKinley, began the reorganization efforts. Under the new organization, the secretary of war reported directly to the president. A new position, chief of staff, ranked under the secretary of war and replaced the existing army commanding general. The chief of staff had a group of officers, called the general staff, as advisers. Root also

★ As the US secretary of war, Elihu Root transformed the army in the early 1900s.

tried to consolidate activities such as payroll and transportation, although some of these took several years to implement. The National Guard, composed of trained militias from each state in the country, was now the reserve for the US Army and could be called into duty by the federal government.

Root's new general staff played a major part in the eventual victory in World War I (1914–1918) for the United States and its allies. The United States entered World War I in 1917 on the side of the Allies, which included France, Great Britain, and Russia. The US Army drafted approximately four million soldiers to fight the war. General John J. Pershing commanded the American Expeditionary Force that landed in France and helped free Europe from the Central Powers of Germany and Austria-Hungary. During World War I, the US Army added several new branches, including the Veterinary Corps and the Chemical Corps. It also added the Aviation Corps, which would later become the US Air Force. New weapon technologies included tanks, machine guns, and airplanes for surveillance.

ELIHU ROOT (1845–1937)

Elihu Root's efforts shaped the modern army and prepared it for the United States' involvement in world affairs. Many of his changes are still in place today, and his reorganization efforts have led many people to consider him one of the most successful US military administrators. Root attended Hamilton College in New York, graduating at age 19. Three years later, he graduated from law school, and by age 30, he had a successful corporate law firm that worked with wealthy clients such as railroads and banks. In 1899, President McKinley appointed him secretary of war and Root began the job of reorganizing the US Army. He founded the War College, expanded the US Military Academy at West Point, and created new procedures for promotions. Under Root, the army became disciplined and strictly organized. In 1905, President Theodore Roosevelt appointed Root as secretary of state. Root was an impressive diplomat, settling disputes and making treaties with countries around the world. Root served as a US senator representing New York from 1909 to 1915. He then continued working in international affairs, trying to create international peace through law rather than war. He received the Nobel Peace Prize in 1912.

WORLD WAR II AND MORE CHANGES

The US Army was a critical part of World War II (1939–1945), a global war between the Allies—which included France, Great Britain, the Soviet Union, and the United States—and the Axis powers, led by Nazi Germany, Italy, and Japan. The United States entered the war in December 1941 after Japan bombed Pearl Harbor, an American naval base in Hawaii. Congress ordered a draft, and the army rapidly expanded to 8.3 million troops. Five million of these served overseas in Europe, North Africa, and the Pacific.[3] General George C. Marshall served as the army chief of staff throughout the war. On June 6, 1944, in the largest amphibious invasion in history, 1.3 million troops landed on the beaches of Normandy, France, to begin retaking Nazi-held Europe.

NISEI SOLDIERS

After the 1941 Japanese military attack on the US naval base at Pearl Harbor, Hawaii, President Franklin D. Roosevelt ordered the incarceration of more than 110,000 people of Japanese descent who lived in the continental United States. Approximately two-thirds of them were American citizens. Many were children of immigrants and were born in the United States. They were called Nisei. Despite widespread prejudice, about 33,000 Nisei joined the US Army. More than 19,000 of them served in three units—the 100th Infantry Battalion, the 442nd Regimental Combat Team, and the Military Intelligence Service. Despite having friends and relatives unfairly treated by their country, these Nisei units were among the most decorated in the war. The three units received the Congressional Gold Medal in 2010.[4]

GEORGE C. MARSHALL (1880–1959)

George C. Marshall, the son of a coal mine owner in Pennsylvania, is remembered not only as one of the greatest US Army soldiers but also as a respected statesman and diplomat. Marshall graduated from the Virginia Military Institute and served as an officer during World War I. In 1939, Marshall accepted the position of US Army chief of staff. He became the army's second five-star general in 1944 and led the largest US Army in history to victory in World War II. Marshall retired from the army after World War II. President Truman appointed Marshall as secretary of state from 1947 to 1949 and as secretary of defense from 1950 to 1951. In 1953, Marshall won the Nobel Peace Prize for leading the European Recovery Program, also known as the Marshall Plan, which is credited with helping restore and maintain democracy in Western Europe.

General Douglas MacArthur, commander of the US Army's forces in the Philippines, fought Japan in the Pacific. Japan surrendered in 1945 after the United States dropped nuclear bombs on the Japanese cities of Hiroshima and Nagasaki. The army innovated with a lot of new technology during the war, such as pressurized airplane cabins, radio navigation and radar, synthetic oil and rubber, jet engines, nuclear weapons, and computers.

The aftermath of World War II brought significant changes to the military, including the army, when Congress passed the National Security Act of 1947. Congress created the Department of Defense to replace the Department of War. To enforce the separation between civilian and military leadership of the army, the secretary of defense was required by law to be a civilian for at least ten years (later reduced to seven years) before taking office. Congress waived this restriction in 1950 for the national hero George C. Marshall, but it was then followed until 2017, when President Donald Trump appointed former marine general James Mattis as secretary of defense. Also under the National Security Act, the US Air Force became a separate military branch, and the Office of Strategic Services became the Central Intelligence Agency (CIA). The act also founded what would become the Army Medical Department and introduced the GI Bill to help the millions of veterans returning to civilian life.

After World War II, the size of the army rapidly decreased. It had three million troops in January 1946 but only 554,000 by March 1948.[5] However, shortly after the war ended, the United States became involved in a different kind of war with the Soviet Union. The Soviet Union had a communist government, and it started taking control of countries in Eastern Europe to establish communist governments there. The United States opposed the Soviets' actions, which resulted in the Cold War (1947–1991). The Cold War didn't involve active fighting. Instead, the United States and the Soviet Union both built up their armies and weapons in preparation for a possible war. The Soviet Union also supported communist forces in Asia, which led to US involvement in the Korean War (1950–1953) and the Vietnam War (1955–1975). The United States drafted young men into the army again, and troop levels returned to more than one million during these two wars.[6] After the United States withdrew from

★ Many Americans protested the Vietnam War and the drafting of soldiers at that time.

Vietnam in 1973, the draft ended. The US military became a voluntary force.

THE WAR ON TERROR

With the fall of the Soviet Union in 1991 and the end of the Cold War, the US Army began to focus more on technology. Satellites could be used both for imaging and for the global positioning system (GPS). GPS is widely used for civilian and military navigation. The Persian Gulf War in 1991 showed the strength of this new high-tech army when the United States and its allies defeated Iraq within weeks. Massive air strikes were followed by an invasion of 700,000 troops, 540,000 of whom were from the United States.[7]

The US military soon faced a new challenge—terrorism. On September 11, 2001, foreign terrorists hijacked four commercial airplanes. They crashed two of these into the World Trade Center towers in New York City and another into the Pentagon, the headquarters of the US Department of Defense, in Washington, DC. Nearly 3,000 people were killed.[8] The fourth airplane headed for the White House, but as passengers fought back against the hijackers, it crashed in a field in Pennsylvania before reaching its target. This attack prompted the War on Terror, an effort to capture and destroy terrorists who threaten the United States and its allies. The War on Terror led to wars

★ The World Trade Center, a complex of buildings that included two skyscrapers known as the Twin Towers, burned over New York City during the terrorist attacks of September 11, 2001.

★ Even as they are trained in the latest technologies and strategies, today's US Army soldiers still follow long-lived military traditions, such as the salute.

in Afghanistan, Iraq, and Syria. Instead of drafting troops, the United States called on its reserves, especially the National Guard, to fill active duty army positions. Although combat missions officially ended in 2014 in Afghanistan, peacekeeping efforts continued there in 2019.

THE MODERN ARMY

As of 2019, the US Army had more than 700,000 troops in active duty or reserves.[9] They are charged with supporting international alliances such as the North Atlantic Treaty Organization (NATO), defending allies such as South Korea and Japan, participating in ongoing peacekeeping efforts around the world, and securing the US borders, including stopping illegal drugs from being transported into the country.

Today's soldiers have high-tech gear to protect them in combat. Advanced weapons and equipment make for a formidable fighting force. Technology such as drones for reconnaissance gives army commanders better information for offensive and defensive missions in the field. Drones carrying weapons also provide a method of fighting from a distance.

As warfare changes, the army adapts. In 2010, the army established the US Army Cyber Command. It handles cyberspace operations, which include protecting the United States from electronic attack, waging electronic warfare, and maintaining cyber communications and information systems for the United States and its allies.

CHAPTER 3

THE US ARMY TODAY

T he army is the largest of the six branches of the US military, which also includes the US Air Force, US Navy, US Marine Corps, US Coast Guard, and US Space Force. Each branch is organized under the US Department of Defense except for the coast guard, which is under the Department of Homeland Security. The US president serves as the commander in chief of the entire US military. He or she appoints, and the

A US Army major general, *right*, visits a ship of an allied country. Sometimes US military personnel work closely with militaries from other countries.

Senate approves, a civilian secretary of defense to oversee the military. An army general called the chief of staff leads the army. He or she is the official military adviser to the secretary of the army, the secretary of defense, the president, and the National Security Council, which is composed of additional military advisers to the president.

In addition to active soldiers, the army has two reserves of personnel that it can call into active duty. The US Army Reserve is owned and maintained by the federal government.

The National Guard is divided into units that are owned and maintained by each state, but the army can call National Guard units into service for the federal government if needed. The army also has special operations forces units, known as the Army Rangers and the Green Berets. These highly trained special operations units are deployed for covert missions such as hostage rescue, reconnaissance, or anti-terrorism missions. They may be involved in unconventional warfare, such as helping resistance groups overcome corrupt foreign governments.

RANKS

Army soldiers are organized by rank. Those of higher rank have the authority to give orders to those of lower rank. This helps maintain an orderly chain of command. The three broad categories of rank are enlisted soldiers, warrant officers, and commissioned officers. Enlisted soldiers are in the lower ranks and serve in every area of the army. Enlisted soldiers can be promoted to higher ranks, becoming noncommissioned officers (NCOs). Warrant officers are experts and trainers in a technical field. Some warrant officers serve as army pilots. Commissioned officers make plans, give orders, and assign enlisted soldiers to jobs. They are also battlefield leaders and fighting soldiers themselves.

★ New soldiers are sworn into the army under oath before they join the lowest ranks.

As soldiers move up in rank, they supervise those with lower ranks and take on more responsibilities. Among enlisted soldiers, there are nine ranks, from private to sergeant major. No matter what army job a soldier has, rank and years of service determine the soldier's base pay. Although base pay is the same across all members of the military, it's also possible to receive special pay for skills or talents that contribute to a specific job.

Army pay grades are designated as E-1 to E-9. Pay grades E-1 to E-3 are privates, E-4 are corporals or specialists, and grades E-5 to E-9 are noncommissioned officers at various levels of sergeant. Enlisted soldiers enter the army as privates (E-1). Unit commanders decide when each soldier is promoted, but after six months, privates generally are promoted to E-2. Later, often

The army holds ceremonies to promote soldiers to higher ranks. ★

after four months, they are promoted to private first class (E-3). After two years of service, an E-3 can move up to specialist or corporal (E-4). Moving to higher ranks depends on qualifications and what job openings are available. To be promoted to officers' ranks, enlisted soldiers must obtain a bachelor's degree and complete officer training.

Warrant officers outrank all enlisted NCOs. They are technical professionals such as military police or intelligence officers. Those who are staff sergeants (E-6) and higher may be chosen to attend the Warrant Officer Candidate School. There, they receive leadership training as well as advanced training in their areas of expertise.

KEEP LEARNING

Army service requires continuous learning, and the army sends experienced soldiers to schools throughout their careers. For example, the army has schools for new sergeants and schools for future battalion commanders. The most senior school is the Army War College in Carlisle, Pennsylvania. The Army War College was established in 1901 to train staff and to advise the president by devising plans and tactics and directing army intelligence. After World War I, the college's focus became more academic. Students including future generals George Patton and Dwight D. Eisenhower, who later served as US president, studied the history of war and its social and political aspects. After World War II, the focus again shifted to the practical aspects of war. Today, the War College is an international experience. Approximately 80 senior military officials from around the world are invited to attend the War College to study alongside US military personnel.

MILITARY OCCUPATIONAL SPECIALTIES

Army enlistees are required to have a high school diploma or a general equivalency diploma (GED). Those with a GED may be required to have a few college credits, so it's generally easier to enlist with a high school diploma instead of a GED. Enlisted soldiers are trained in jobs called military occupational specialties (MOS). More than 150 MOS are available in the army. A soldier's MOS is determined by his or her interests and aptitude for a particular job.

ARMY PAY

The amount of money a soldier earns depends on his or her rank, time in service, and specific talents, training, or abilities. As of late 2019, E-1 soldiers received $1,732.94 per month base pay. Soldiers who achieved the E-9 pay grade after 20 years of service received $6,419.88 per month. A commissioned officer began at $3,287.35 per month and after 20 years of service could achieve a pay grade of O-9 and receive $15,905.70 per month. Soldiers deployed overseas get slightly more pay. In addition to pay, soldiers receive benefits such as housing and medical insurance. National Guard and reserve soldiers, unless they are called to active duty, are paid for monthly drill duty and weeklong drill periods. They typically have a separate nonmilitary career. As of late 2019, E-1 soldiers in the reserves and National Guard received $231.06 per month. Officers started at $438.31 per month. Soldiers are also able to earn extra bonuses for enlisting in areas that are in high demand.[1]

A soldier's MOS is designated by a number followed by a letter. The number in an MOS represents a family of jobs, and the letter represents a specific job within that family. For example, 13 is the family number for field artillery. A 13B is a cannon crewmember, while a 13E is a cannon fire direction specialist. Soldiers with a 13E MOS develop the information needed to hit targets and provide that information to the gun crews. The army uses the International Radiotelephony Spelling Alphabet, also called the NATO phonetic alphabet, for MOS letters. In this alphabet, for example, a 13B is called a "13 Bravo" while a 13E is a "13 Echo."

Upon entering the army, recruits take the Armed Services Vocational Aptitude Battery (ASVAB) to determine their eligibility for particular jobs. The test is divided into subject areas including general science, arithmetic reasoning, word knowledge, paragraph comprehension, mathematics knowledge, auto and shop information, mechanical comprehension, assembling objects, and electronic information. The highest possible overall score on the ASVAB is 99, and the minimum score for enlistment is 31. The ASVAB has individual section scores that are combined in different ways to determine line scores, which may be higher than 99. Line scores determine which MOS a recruit may qualify for. Each MOS has different requirements for line scores.

THE TOP RANKS

Commissioned officers, the top-ranking personnel in the army, are college-educated administrators of the army. There are several ways to become a commissioned officer. They are by attending Officer Candidate School, Reserve Officers Training Corps (ROTC), or US Military Academy, or by receiving direct commissions for certain professions.

The Officer Candidate School course is open to active and reserve soldiers and civilians. Applicants must be 19 to 32 years old, have a four-year college degree, and be eligible for a secret security clearance. All applicants must complete basic combat training. This 12-week course teaches leadership skills.

A second pathway to becoming an officer is ROTC. In addition to academic college classes, ROTC students take elective classes that prepare them for becoming an army officer. They also attend summer camps. The ROTC program provides money to pay for college tuition as well as a stipend for living expenses. Upon successful completion of the program, ROTC cadets are commissioned as army officers. They agree to serve eight years in the army, which may consist of active and/or reserve service. In addition to paying for college, ROTC aims to help students develop leadership skills and other traits that will be useful in civilian jobs after their army service. Major Otto Padron, an army reserve infantry officer who attended ROTC to pay for college,

US ARMY RANKS

ENLISTED SOLDIERS

Private
Private Second Class
Private First Class
Specialist

NONCOMMISSIONED OFFICERS (ENLISTED)

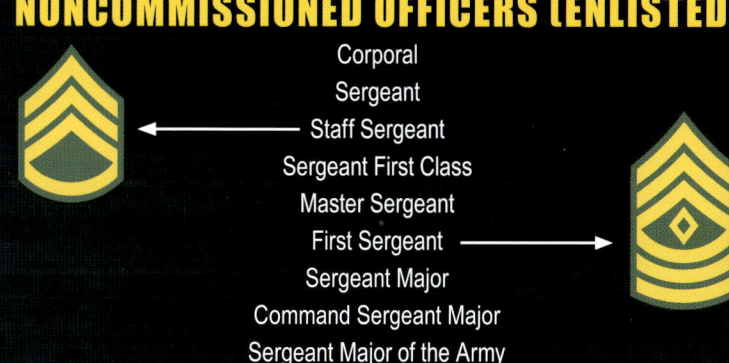

Corporal
Sergeant
Staff Sergeant
Sergeant First Class
Master Sergeant
First Sergeant
Sergeant Major
Command Sergeant Major
Sergeant Major of the Army

WARRANT OFFICERS

Warrant Officer 1
Chief Warrant Officer 2
Chief Warrant Officer 3
Chief Warrant Officer 4
Chief Warrant Officer 5

COMMISSIONED OFFICERS

Second Lieutenant
First Lieutenant
Captain
Major
Lieutenant Colonel
Colonel
Brigadier General
Major General
Lieutenant General
General

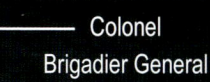

SECURITY CLEARANCES

Depending on a soldier's role in the US Army, he or she may be required to see sensitive information that, if known by enemies, could be damaging to the security of the country. MOS that require the use of sensitive data must pass a background check to obtain a security clearance. The three main levels of security clearance are confidential, secret, and top secret. Confidential means that disclosing information could cause damage to national security. Secret means that disclosing information could cause serious damage to security, while top secret means that disclosing information could have exceptionally grave consequences to national security. The Department of Defense has its own security system that investigates criminal, financial, and psychological information to give soldiers security clearances. The lower security clearances require investigation of the past five years of a person's history, while a top-secret clearance requires investigating ten years of a person's history. It also involves personal interviews with references such as former employers. Security clearances must be updated periodically.

says, "Army strong, to me, meant that if you were good, you were going to be the best."[2]

A third path to becoming an officer is by attending the US Military Academy at West Point. This prestigious college is open to students ages 17 to 22 who are single and not pregnant or responsible for child support. Selection is extremely rigorous.

Professionals such as doctors or lawyers may receive a direct commission as an officer when joining the army. Many of these professionals are non-line officers who cannot command combat troops.

Commissioned officers move up through ranks of lieutenant, captain, major, lieutenant colonel, colonel, and then five levels

★ In addition to training in the field, army training includes education in classrooms.

of generals. The lowest rank of general is a one-star general. A star is added for each increase in rank. By law, the army has only seven positions for four-star generals. The rank of five-star general is usually only given in times of war. Base pay for officers is designated with pay grades O-1 to O-10.

ORGANIZATION OF UNITS

Army members are organized into units of increasing size. As the number of members in a unit increases, the unit has more responsibility and is led by a higher-ranking soldier. The smallest group is the fire team, often composed of four soldiers—two

WOMEN IN THE ARMY

Although women served in the army as nurses and seamstresses beginning with the American Revolution, they did not serve in large numbers until World War II. In addition to serving in the new Army Nursing Corps of that time, approximately 25,000 women served overseas as secretaries, telephone operators, administrators, and in other noncombat positions. Also during World War II, 140,000 women served in the newly formed Women's Army Corps (WAC). They worked in hundreds of different areas, from collecting military intelligence to rigging parachutes. More than 1,000 women served as Women Airforce Service Pilots (WASP), flying military airplanes to where they were needed for maintenance or tactical support. After World War II, WAC leaders worked to equalize men's and women's roles in the army. By 1967, women could join the National Guard and pay was equalized for officers. A decade later, MOS training was integrated for men and women. Gradually more jobs opened to women, with all MOS open to them by 2016.[3]

riflemen, a grenadier, and an automatic rifleman. One of the soldiers, usually a sergeant or corporal, is the leader. Fire team leaders are responsible for the soldiers in a fire team, making sure that every member has the equipment and knowledge needed for each assignment. Some fire teams may have specialists in communications or special systems such as the Stinger, a shoulder-fired antiaircraft missile.

A squad consists of four to ten soldiers and is led by a sergeant. Three or four squads (16 to 44 soldiers) form a platoon, which is led by a lieutenant. Three to five platoons (60 to 200 soldiers) form a company, which is led by a captain. Some companies have special names. In artillery units, which operate big guns, companies are called batteries. In armored units, such as tank units and air cavalry, companies are called troops. Four to six companies (300 to 1,000 soldiers) form a battalion, commanded by a lieutenant colonel. Two to five battalions form a brigade (1,500 to 3,200 soldiers), which is led by a colonel. Three brigades form a division (10,000 to 16,000 soldiers), led by a major general. Two to five divisions form a corps (20,000 to 45,000 soldiers), led by a lieutenant general. The largest group is a field army, consisting of more than 50,000 soldiers led by a lieutenant general or higher-ranking general.[4]

WELCOME ★★ TO BASIC

BECOMING ARMY STRONG

Basic combat training, or boot camp, is a ten-week course that makes enlistees into soldiers. The course has three phases—Red, White, and Blue. It isn't easy. Trainees are physically and mentally challenged to be the absolute best they can be.

Boot camp begins with meeting the drill sergeant, who is responsible for teaching enlistees to act like soldiers, including how to dress, how to address superiors, and how to work on a team. During the introductory Red Phase, enlistees can expect exhausting physical exertion as they exercise, march, and run to increase their stamina and strength. They memorize the Soldier's Creed, which lists the standards by which all soldiers are expected to conduct themselves. Completion of the Red Phase results in earning an Army Unit Patch, the insignia worn on the left sleeve to signify a soldier's unit.

The White Phase is the introduction to marksmanship and maintaining a weapon. Enlistees learn hand-to-hand combat and continue their physical training. They navigate obstacle courses and rappel from the 50-foot (15 m) Warrior Tower.

In the Blue Phase, enlistees continue physical training and marksmanship. They learn to use more advanced weapons such as machine guns and live grenades as well as how to locate and disable IEDs. They work with a team in convoys and in tactical maneuvers. The final test requires the trainees to navigate a simulated combat course over multiple days. This course tests their physical fitness and skills. When a trainee passes these boot camp challenges, he or she receives the black beret of a US Army soldier. Then the soldier can move forward with his or her career in the army.

★ A drill sergeant monitors recruits during basic combat training.

CHAPTER 4

INFANTRY

The infantry (MOS 11X) is the backbone of the army. It is the frontline fighting force, defending the country by land and capturing, destroying, or repelling enemy forces in combat. Approximately 15 to 17 percent of the army is infantry.[1]

Infantry soldiers have a wide range of duties and responsibilities. They may do reconnaissance or locate and neutralize land mines. They set up defensive perimeters or

Infantry soldiers are trained for different types of combat, such as raids on enemy headquarters.

offensive preparations for moving larger weapons. This job may require radio communication skills and map reading skills.

Infantry soldiers must always be prepared to engage enemy combatants during any hour of the day. Night vision goggles help infantrymen perform missions in darkness. Depending on their skills and knowledge, they may be part of a fire team during an attack or defensive situation. Infantrymen must properly process captured prisoners and ensure that any captured sensitive documents are quickly provided to intelligence specialists.

Although the army has a huge team of experts to support the infantry, from mechanics to systems analysts, it is up to these frontline troops to use those resources to their best advantage. They evaluate terrain and provide that information on maps for analysts to use in making decisions on troop strengths and placement. During combat, they may call for additional direct or indirect fire or adjust fire for the situation and movements of the enemy. They may also construct temporary barricades, control the inflow and storage of ammunition, or provide first aid to casualties.

THE INFANTRY AT HOME

The army provides housing for active duty infantry even when they are not deployed. Housing depends on a soldier's rank, MOS, location, and family size. A single soldier of a lower rank may live on an army post in the barracks, which are apartments with private bedrooms and a kitchen shared with roommates. Facilities often have mudrooms where infantrymen can clean muddy boots and equipment after field exercises. Accommodations are larger for married soldiers. Soldiers with children live in condos or houses large enough to accommodate their children. Army family housing may be houses with yards in communities with parks, a pool, and other amenities. Not all army personnel are required to live on army posts. If they live off post, they are provided with a housing allowance.

Infantrymen are the boots on the ground, ready to do whatever tasks are required to defeat the enemy. They travel on foot, in armored vehicles, or over land in helicopters. They are ready for field combat in various terrains

★ Infantry soldiers work to make sure they're a solid team on the battlefield.

or urban combat in towns and cities. They are trained to respond to nuclear, biological, or chemical threats. They are prepared to use rifles, grenades, machine guns, mines, and light anti-tank weapons if needed. They are also trained in first aid.

ARMY GEAR

A US soldier carries at least 60 pounds (27 kg) of gear, and often much more. The combat army uniform, including gloves, boots, and glasses, weighs less than ten pounds (4.5 kg). But additional protective gear adds a lot of weight. A tactical vest that protects against bullets and shrapnel adds about 30 pounds (14 kg), and the helmet adds another three pounds (1.4 kg). Over the tactical vest is another vest for carrying ammunition, a first aid kit, water, grenades, and whatever other equipment or weapons the soldier needs. An additional rucksack to hold supplies may weigh between 20 and 100 pounds (9 and 45 kg), depending on the duration of the mission. Soldiers may also need cold weather gear, chemical masks, or other specialty equipment. Modern soldiers also need electronics, such as night vision goggles, scopes, communications devices, and flashlights. These may require up to 16 pounds (7 kg) of batteries.[2]

When not actively engaged in combat, infantry personnel are training. They must hone their skills and learn new weapons, equipment, and tactics. They must stay in top physical shape to be ready for deployment at a moment's notice. Infantry soldiers in the National Guard are also on the front lines to assist states during hurricanes, floods, and other emergencies.

SKILLS AND TRAINING

Infantry is a good career choice for people interested in light weapons and fighting with ground troops. Successful infantry personnel must be disciplined, ready to accept danger, and able to deal with stressful situations. Physically, they must be in excellent shape and able to lift more than 100 pounds (45 kg).

They should also be able to lift 50 pounds (23 kg) regularly. They often work outdoors in harsh field conditions. They must be able to work with a team.

Infantry requires a score of at least 87 in combat on the ASVAB. Training as MOS 11X teaches an enlistee to work as an infantryman (11B) or indirect fire infantryman (11C). MOS 11B works with direct fire weapons such as rifles, while 11C works with indirect fire weapons such as mortars. Although candidates may request either 11B or 11C, positions may not always be open in the desired area. Upon completion of 11X training, the soldiers are assigned to 11B or 11C, depending on where they are needed.

MAKING AN IMPACT

The infantry is a major focus of the US Army. Without these soldiers to carry out the tasks on the ground, all of the army's advanced equipment, weapons, analysis, and tactical planning would have no purpose. The infantry is the front line in defeating the enemy. When infantry members do their jobs well, it can mean victory, while mistakes can cost lives and lead to defeat. The infantry is the face of the army. It is the first to enter new territory and make an impression on the civilian population. As such, its soldiers represent the United States with their professionalism and strength. Infantry soldiers must be disciplined, strong, and able to withstand the stress of the battlefield and many hours in the field. Ultimately, they win or lose battles for the United States.

Infantry soldiers practice at a shooting range. ★

Infantry training combines boot camp with Advanced Individual Training. As of 2019, a program called Infantry One Station Unit Training was expanded from 14 weeks to 22 weeks. The original 14-week training included physical defense, weapons training, and tactical field training in mines and other combat skills. The additional training has more emphasis on hand-to-hand combat, lifesaving skills during combat, day and night navigation, and qualifications on various weapons including the M4 rifle, M240 machine gun, and M249 squad automatic weapon. Captain Richard Taylor trains soldiers. He says, "My goal is to fight and

US ARMY DRILL TEAM AND THE OLD GUARD

The US Army Drill Team is an elite, ceremonial platoon that serves as an ambassador for the US Army nationally and internationally. It also supports army recruitment and community relations. The drill team's 19 members perform precise maneuvers using bayonet-tipped 1903 Springfield rifles. Their performances feature synchronized movements, marching, and rifle handling. Drill team members are selected after six months of drill practice. They must have good bearing, strength, and dexterity.

The drill team is a platoon in the 3rd US Infantry Regiment, also known as the Old Guard. The Old Guard, founded in 1784, is the oldest active infantry regiment. Old Guard members provide security for Washington, DC, in times of emergency. They act in ceremonies at national monuments and escort the president. They also escort funerals at Arlington National Cemetery and guard the Tomb of the Unknown Soldier, a monument dedicated to deceased soldiers whose remains were never identified.

win in combat. We take them through hard training, realistic training, and focused training."[3]

The skills that infantry soldiers learn can help them get jobs in the civilian world. Infantrymen may enroll in the Army PaYS Program, which matches former soldiers with large civilian companies that are seeking workers. Many large companies seek workers with skills learned in the military, such as discipline and a strong work ethic. The PaYS Program ensures a veteran at least one interview with a participating company.

TOP FIVE QUESTIONS

★ CAN SOMEONE ENLIST IN THE INFANTRY WHILE THEY ARE STILL IN HIGH SCHOOL?

The army has a delayed entry program that allows a person to enlist and begin active service up to a year later, which allows someone to enlist while in high school and then begin serving after graduation. Whether recruits can serve in the infantry depends on their qualifications, including their ASVAB scores.

★ WILL THE ARMY PAY FOR COLLEGE FOR A PERSON WHO JOINS THE INFANTRY?

Under the GI Bill, all soldiers who have served on active duty for at least 90 days are eligible for money for college tuition. Soldiers may also be eligible for textbook and housing allowances. The amount of funding received depends on how long a soldier serves. A soldier who serves two years receives full tuition at state universities.

★ ASIDE FROM INFANTRY, WHAT OTHER COMBAT JOBS ARE AVAILABLE?

For those wanting to be on the front line, there are many specialized MOS positions available. All advanced offensive or defensive equipment requires special training. These MOS include armor crewmen (19K), who are part of a tank team; cavalry scouts (19D), who move ahead of their units to spy on enemy combatants and report back to commanders; cannon crewmembers (13B), who fire cannons; and others who work with missile launch systems.

★ HOW LONG DO INFANTRYMEN ENLIST FOR?

Most army enlistments are for eight years. Four years are generally active duty. The remaining four years are in the Individual Ready Reserve. These inactive reserves may be called up in times of personnel shortages, war, or other emergencies. The army offers a few active enlistment periods of two years for hard-to-fill positions.

★ WHAT CIVILIAN JOBS WILL AN INFANTRYMAN BE TRAINED FOR?

Although many infantry skills are specialized to army combat and cannot be directly applied to the civilian workforce, infantrymen can use some of their skills by working in security or law enforcement.

CHAPTER 5

GEOSPATIAL INTELLIGENCE IMAGERY ANALYST

Geospatial intelligence imagery analysts (MOS 35G) take information from maps, digital images taken by satellites, or other aerial images. They then analyze the data to help

Geospatial intelligence imagery analysts must have good computer skills.

field army commanders determine battlefield conditions and the strength and position of enemy forces. They also provide support to combat troops in the field and to those who plan reconnaissance or surveillance missions. One MOS 35G soldier explains, "We are the eyes in the sky. We tell the commanders what they need to know. They make the big decisions with the information we give them."[1]

A geospatial intelligence imagery analyst may work in the field with combat troops. At an entry level (35G10), the analyst examines data from many sources, including radar, infrared imaging, and normal photographs. Analysts use computers, visual cues, or stereoscopes to identify military installations and equipment. Stereoscopes show side-by-side photographs to help the analyst view the image in three dimensions. Using stereoscopic vision helps analysts identify structures and calculate the size of objects such as buildings or missile silos.

During and after combat operations, analysts work to assess battle damages caused by enemies and the US Army itself. The analysts create maps and write their assessments in battle damage reports. Analysts also take data from sources in the field, such as reports from scouts, to create hand-drawn or computer maps. They overlay these maps with earlier aerial images to determine changes in the landscape. During combat missions, this information

WHAT'S A STEREOSCOPE?

A stereoscope is an instrument that allows the viewer to look at flat photographs of an object and see the object in 3-D. People normally see in 3-D because each eye views an object from a slightly different angle. The images then come together in the brain to produce depth of vision so that objects look three-dimensional. Stereoscopes provide a way to see this 3-D effect on flat photographs. Two pictures are taken of an object, such as a tower, from slightly different angles. The angles correspond to how each eye would view the object in the real world. Looking through the stereoscope combines these views to form a 3-D image of the object. In spatial analysis, using a stereoscope makes it easier to identify objects and measure their width and height.

must be accessed quickly, analyzed accurately, and reported immediately to commanders who are assessing situations that are changing by the minute. Field conditions are often stressful, but image analysts are prepared to set up and work under these conditions to deliver intelligence.

At the next level, 35G20, analysts assess the best approaches for soldiers moving into position and perform more in-depth assessments of battle damages. They also create more in-depth reports and maps. They supervise those at lower ranks to ensure that work is moving forward. At higher levels, 35G30 and 35G40, analysts help target enemy combatants in the field and monitor increases in enemy weapons. They support intelligence operations and the delivery of images and reports at all levels along the chain of command. At the highest levels, analysts may work at the National Geospatial Intelligence Agency with

MAKING AN IMPACT

Gathering, analyzing, and reporting intelligence is a vital role in the army. Today's high-tech army has tools such as satellites and drones that can gather data from multiple sources in a variety of formats, from satellite images to aerial photographs. However, this data has to be properly analyzed and reported in a timely manner for it to be useful, and it takes skill to interpret data from these sources. Commanders are dependent on the information gathered and reported by geospatial analysts to make decisions that affect the lives of soldiers and the army's success in battle.

civilians and specialists from other military branches. These analysts write reports of their findings.

SKILLS AND TRAINING

Besides being interested in reading maps and gathering and analyzing spatial data, analysts must have good communication skills. They must speak and write concisely because the information they provide is vital to army missions. Applicants must take a vision test and a hearing test. Normal color vision is essential. Applicants must also be able to use a stereoscopic tool to visualize images in three dimensions.

GLOBAL POSITIONING SYSTEM

Analysts depend on the global positioning system (GPS) to accurately plot positions on maps. The GPS, owned by the United States, uses a system of satellites that sends signals to Earth. The satellites are positioned so that receivers on the ground can pick up multiple signals at once. Receivers pick up the signals and calculate the time it took for each signal to travel from each satellite, which tells the receiver the distance to a satellite. Using signals from three satellites, a receiver can use triangulation to calculate its position on Earth. The accuracy of a GPS coordinate depends on the receiver, ground conditions, and access to different signals from the satellites. The GPS on a smartphone is accurate to about a 16-foot (4.9 m) radius under good conditions. High-end GPS, using the precise positioning system frequencies available only to the US military and certain other countries, can locate a position to within a few centimeters and make long-term measurements, such as movement of land masses, within millimeters.

★ Analysts may work in offices or in the field.

Due to the highly sensitive nature of the information an analyst reviews, an MOS 35G needs a top-secret security clearance from the Department of Defense. A soldier applying for this position will have his or her background checked, including financial, criminal, and drug activity. Any convictions by court martial or in civil court, except for minor traffic matters, will prevent an applicant from getting the job. To work as a 35G, a soldier must be a US citizen and all of his or her immediate relatives must also be US citizens.

Requirements for intelligence jobs such as MOS 35G are very strict. For example, to obtain an army intelligence job, applicants, their immediate families, and families of their spouses cannot live in or have financial interests in a foreign country where physical or mental coercion is commonly used.

To be accepted in this MOS, applicants must have an ASVAB score of 101 in skilled technician. The army prefers applicants for this MOS who have two years of previous training or experience in a related field such as cartography, surveying, geology, or aerial photography. Army training for the job includes ten weeks of basic combat training and 22 weeks of Advanced Individual Training at Fort Huachuca in Arizona. Part of the training is in a classroom, and other parts are in the field. Students learn to access and process a variety of types of images to create intelligence products such as maps and reports.

TOP FIVE QUESTIONS

★ **WHAT OTHER ARMY CAREERS ARE SIMILAR TO GEOSPATIAL INTELLIGENCE IMAGERY ANALYST?**

Geospatial engineers (12Y) use geographic information and geospatial images to support civilian and military efforts for disaster relief and the Department of Homeland Security.

★ **WHAT SHOULD PEOPLE WHO WANT TO BECOME GEOSPATIAL INTELLIGENCE IMAGERY ANALYSTS STUDY IN HIGH SCHOOL?**

This job requires at least one year of high school algebra or geometry.

★ **CAN PEOPLE DO THIS JOB IN THE NATIONAL GUARD?**

MOS 35G is open to enlisted soldiers, active National Guard members, and army reserve soldiers.

★ **WHAT GOVERNMENT JOBS OUTSIDE OF THE ARMY USE GEOSPATIAL ANALYSTS?**

Government intelligence agencies use geospatial intelligence to help inform policymakers' decisions. For example, the National Geospatial-Intelligence Agency is mostly staffed by civilians, even though it supports the army under the Department of Defense.

★ **WHAT CIVILIAN CAREERS DOES THIS ARMY JOB PROVIDE TRAINING FOR?**

Analysts have many opportunities in civilian business and research. They can work as cartographers, surveyors, or map technicians.

CHAPTER 6

CONSTRUCTION EQUIPMENT REPAIRER

Army engineers build roads, bridges, housing, and field headquarters. Anyone who has passed by a large construction site has seen the many types of heavy equipment required for basic construction—earthmoving and loading equipment such as bulldozers, backhoes, and cranes;

Graders are just one type of the many large construction vehicles that MOS 91L soldiers repair and maintain.

equipment for laying foundations or roads such as compacting equipment and cement mixers; and pumping equipment for water and air compression. The army uses these machines and others to extract and crush rocks and to lay asphalt. Construction equipment repairers (MOS 91L) ensure that the construction equipment these soldiers need is maintained, repaired, and ready for action 24 hours a day.

An MOS 91L soldier works in the field anywhere that army construction engineers need heavy equipment. A day begins

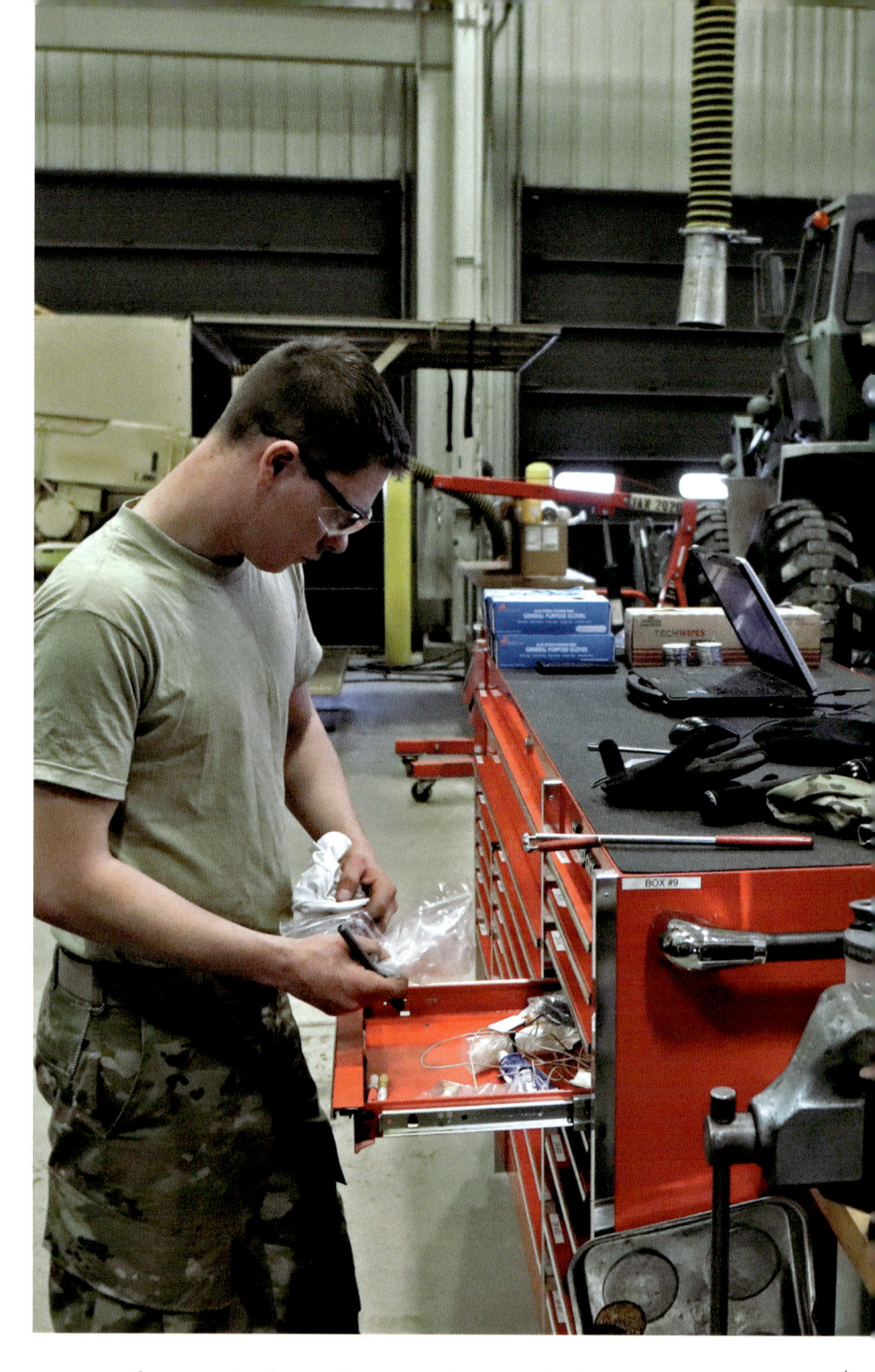

Army construction equipment repairers must be familiar with a wide variety ★
of tools and equipment.

with maintenance, making sure equipment is in good working order, fluids are maintained, and hydraulics and electrical systems are checked. Maintaining construction equipment means that soldiers must be familiar with all the systems in each machine. They may service a backhoe that needs new brakes, replace the alternator in a bulldozer, use equipment to diagnose electronic problems in a crane, or read technical diagrams called schematics to diagnose problems on a rock crusher. There is always work to do, whether it's at a large construction field site or in a maintenance shed at a barracks. In urgent situations,

 ## MAKING AN IMPACT

An MOS 91L's troubleshooting, problem-solving, and hands-on repair skills are vital to keep the army moving. Without these soldiers, the billions of dollars the army invests in equipment, from bulldozers to specialized trucks, would be useless. These soldiers must do their work accurately to keep from endangering a mission. They must be prepared to troubleshoot on a moment's notice. Movement of troops and supplies is essential to support a mission. For people who love machines, there is great satisfaction in taking apart a complex piece of equipment and making it move again. Sergeant First Class Joshua Watson, who trains soldiers for MOS 91L, said, "There's nowhere in the United States, or otherwise, that you're not going to need a construction equipment repairer. Everywhere you go, this job will follow you, and you can take it and be successful, whether you decide to stay in the military and make it a career or you transfer out. It's a phenomenal skill to have, both in the military and out."[1]

a 91L remains on call, day or night, to diagnose or fix any problems that could stop the mission from progressing.

TECHNOLOGY: MAINTENANCE SUPPORT DEVICE

The US Army has hundreds of vehicles, weapon systems, and communications systems that are maintained and repaired by soldiers in a variety of MOS. Information for doing these jobs is available on the maintenance support device (MSD), a computer system containing information on caring for army equipment. Those training for MOS 91 positions must learn to use the MSD to test and identify problems on military equipment. Companies such as Caterpillar that make construction equipment can link their own online support tools to the MSD. Construction equipment repairers can use the system in conjunction with manuals to fix a problem faster.

In addition to maintaining the equipment for the army's construction engineers, a 91L is a soldier who is prepared to pick up a weapon and fight at any time. A 91L must stay in good physical shape, which means physical training every day. These soldiers must maintain their own equipment and continue combat training such as marksmanship.

More advanced 91L grades supervise entry-level soldiers, making sure they maintain discipline and training standards. They work on advanced equipment systems and help lower-rank soldiers identify and fix problems with their equipment. They may have to completely overhaul an engine or use welding equipment to make repairs to metal parts such as fenders or doors. MOS 91L30 grades supervise and inspect repairs, in addition to working on advanced systems.

A special unit of the 91L is the multi-role bridge company. This unit builds bridges to move soldiers and equipment across rivers, lakes, or other bodies of water where there is no bridge or an existing bridge that is not safe. They may build a floating bridge for troops or a bridge to move tanks. The unit uses specialized equipment and trucks to quickly lay pontoons across the water and latch them together into a bridge to keep the soldiers moving. The unit also helps the National Guard in cases of natural disaster, such as hurricanes or floods. The bridges transport people out of or supplies into affected areas that are cut off by water.

In addition to 91L, the army has many other mechanic and repair positions. These all have individual letters under MOS 91. People in these jobs may repair tanks and armored vehicles, work on utilities and power generators, repair weapons, or work as machinists who make parts. Some soldiers are trained on very specific vehicles such as Abrams Tank Systems (91A) and Bradley Fighting Vehicle Systems (91M).

SKILLS AND TRAINING

MOS 91L is for people who are interested in repairing electrical and mechanical systems. They should have experience using

A soldier in the multi-role bridge company helps guide two pieces of a bridge ★ together during a training exercise for the unit.

tools and basic math skills such as high school algebra in order to read schematics. Entry-level positions do basic maintenance, but as soldiers advance, they will need good problem-solving skills to figure out what is wrong with a piece of machinery and how to fix it. Physical strength is important, as soldiers may have to carry heavy parts.

To be accepted as an MOS 91L, applicants must score a 92 in mechanical maintenance or an 87 in mechanical maintenance and an 85 in general technical on the ASVAB. They should have normal color vision. Training includes ten weeks of basic combat training plus eight weeks of advanced training at Fort Leonard Wood, Missouri.

CONTINUING EDUCATION

The army offers continuing education in particular skills beyond those required by a soldier's MOS. This education is called additional skill identifiers (ASI). These may include courses in leadership, physical training, or skills that enhance a soldier's MOS. Some of these additional skills may be available only to specific MOS that are closely related to the additional skills being trained. Others may be available to any MOS, so soldiers from many areas of expertise may take the same class. The courses are open to active duty soldiers or National Guard members. There are a wide variety of opportunities. For instance, 91L can train for certification as a master fitness trainer, a nonlethal weapons trainer, or a competitive parachutist, among many others.

MOS 91L qualifies for the Army Civilian Acquired Skills Program (ACASP). This program allows people with nonmilitary construction experience to quickly move up to the rank of E-4 (specialist). The program also offers these workers a financial bonus upon enlistment. ACASP qualifications for 91L include two years of experience and/or training in maintenance and repair of gasoline and diesel engines and other equipment. Candidates must also have certifications in professional organizations such as Automotive Service Excellence or the American Federation of Labor and Congress of Industrial Organizations (AFL-CIO), a labor union. Getting this experience and training can provide a big head start in army service.

TOP FIVE QUESTIONS

★ **HOW MUCH MONEY DOES AN ARMY CONSTRUCTION EQUIPMENT REPAIRER MAKE?**

Base pay for all military personnel is based on rank and time in service, regardless of MOS. Additional pay for MOS 91L may come from acquiring special certifications or skills through army classes.

★ **WHAT CAN A HIGH SCHOOL STUDENT DO TO PREPARE FOR WORKING AS A 91L?**

Taking high school algebra class and getting experience in mechanics through jobs or other training is helpful to students interested in MOS 91L.

★ **CAN A 91L SOLDIER CHANGE JOBS TO REPAIR DIFFERENT TYPES OF EQUIPMENT?**

Each type of equipment is a different MOS and requires new certification, but it is possible to have more than one MOS. Many specialties include additional weeks of Advanced Individual Training.

★ **CAN A PERSON DO THIS JOB AS A MEMBER OF THE NATIONAL GUARD?**

This MOS is open to enlisted, active army reserve, and National Guard soldiers.

★ **DOES THIS MOS PREPARE SOLDIERS FOR CIVILIAN CAREERS?**

MOS 91L prepares soldiers for civilian jobs with construction companies, state transportations systems, farm equipment and mining companies, and auto repair shops.

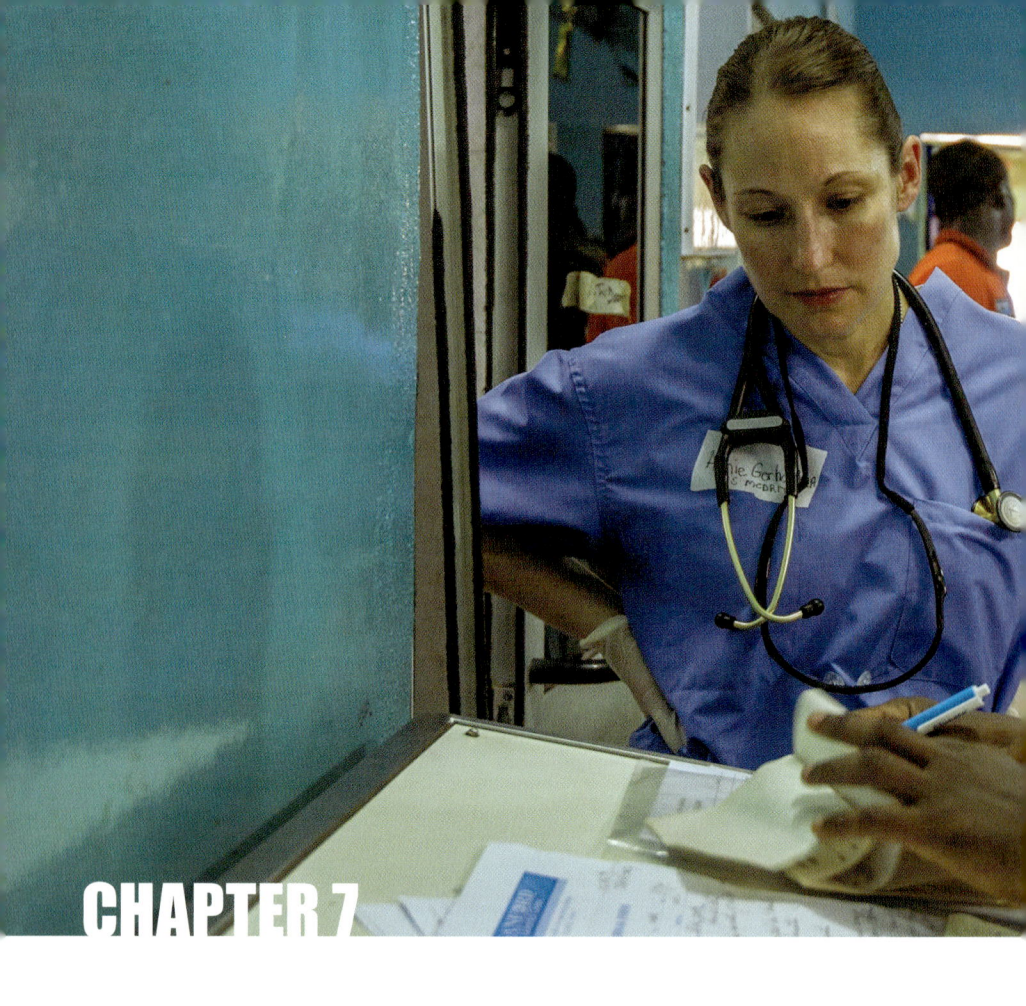

CHAPTER 7

MEDICAL-SURGICAL NURSE

Beginning in the Revolutionary War, many women served the US Army as nurses, although they did not serve in uniform. They served as volunteers in field hospitals caring for the sick and wounded. During the Spanish-American War in 1898, a severe outbreak of typhoid fever made army leaders

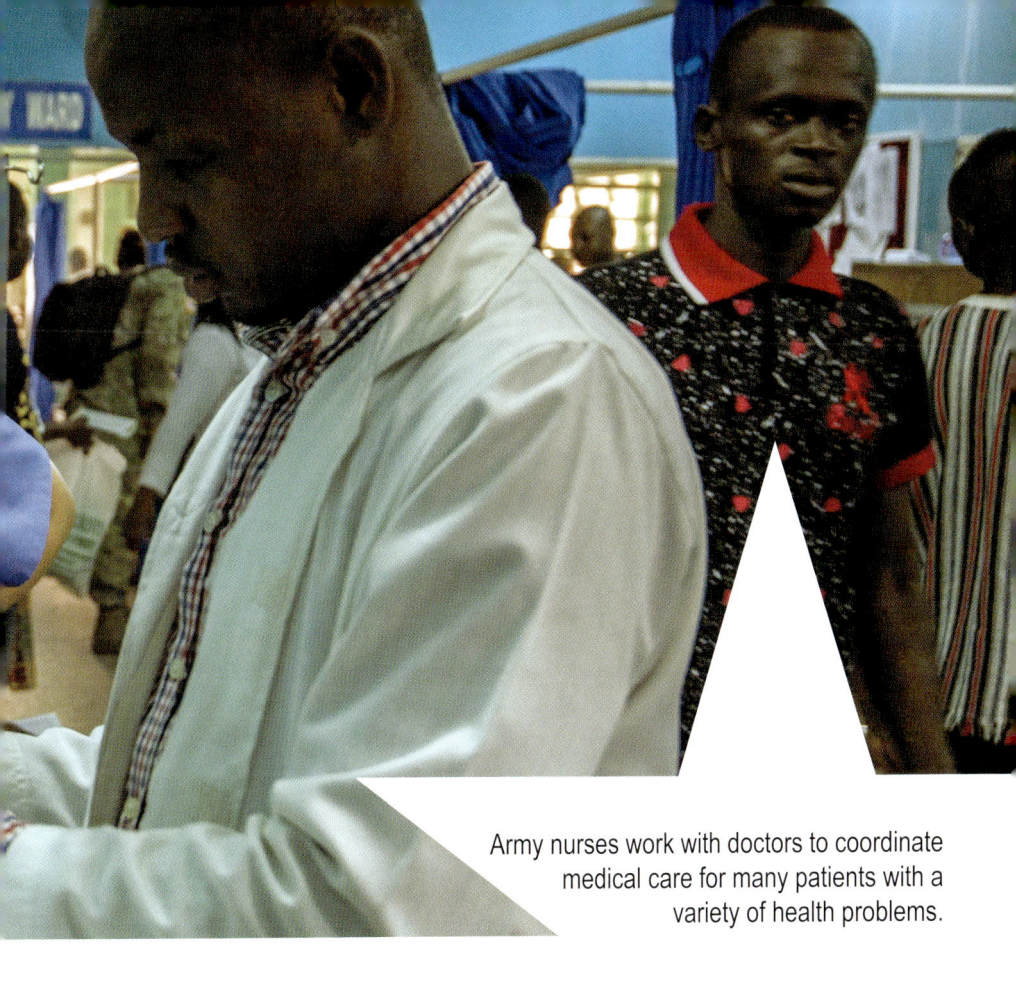

Army nurses work with doctors to coordinate medical care for many patients with a variety of health problems.

realize that official army nurses were needed. The first army nurses contracted with the military served under the direction of the US surgeon general. The assistant surgeon general, Dr. Anita N. McGee, was in charge of recruiting civilian nurses to work with the army. After army leaders realized that they needed an official group of nurses who understood military procedure, Dr. McGee wrote a bill that established the Army Nurse Corps in 1901. One of the army contract nurses, Dita H. Kinney, became the first superintendent of the new unit. It wasn't until 1944 that the US Congress gave army nurses an official role with equal status in rank as soldiers.

Today, the army's medical-surgical nurses (MOS 66H) provide care to a broad range of people, from combat casualties to mothers giving birth. In addition to direct nursing care, they are responsible for storing, preparing, and sterilizing medical equipment. They may also participate in research. Medical-surgical nurses may train other nurses and medical aides for military families who need in-hospital, outpatient, or

DR. ANITA N. MCGEE (1864–1940)

Dr. Anita N. McGee is considered the mother of army nurses. Anita McGee, whose maiden name was Newcomb, was born in 1864 to a wealthy family that encouraged her to pursue education. She attended elite schools in Washington, DC, and took classes in London, England, and Geneva, Switzerland. In 1888, she married William John McGee and soon after began medical school. She graduated from Columbian University, which later became George Washington University. She practiced medicine and pursued her interest in politics through organizations such as the American Association for the Advancement of Science. In 1898, US Army surgeon general George M. Sternberg sent nurses to military bases due to an outbreak of influenza during the Spanish-American War. McGee used her political and organizational skills to encourage Sternberg to send only qualified nurses, helping screen 1,600 nurses for service.[1] Dr. McGee was appointed as assistant surgeon general of the US Army, becoming the only woman at the time to wear an officer's uniform in the army. In 1899, she wrote a military nursing manual. In 1901, she wrote legislation that established the Army Nurse Corps.

MALE NURSES

For many years, only women could serve as army nurses. By the end of World War II, the army and army air force (which is now the US Air Force) had 59,000 nurses.[3] They were all women. In 1949, the US Congress began efforts to allow men into the Army Nurse Corps. Policymakers argued for six years about how this would work, including discussions about whether married men would be accepted, where male nurses would live, whether men would accept orders from women, and how male soldiers would accept male nurses. Finally, in 1955, Congress passed the Bolton Act, which allowed men to join the Army Nurse Corps. Second Lieutenant Edward T. Lyon became the first male nurse commissioned in the Army Nurse Corps later that year. His commission paved the way for other male nurses, who had until that time served as lower-ranked pharmacy technicians or orderlies. Today, women still make up the majority of army nurses, but there is a much larger percentage of male nurses in the army than in civilian medical facilities. As of 2017, 35 percent of army nurses were men.[4] Approximately 11 percent of civilian nurses were men.[5]

home care. Being an army nurse, says Captain Lisa Kasper, "comes with the great pleasure of knowing that I am endorsing a higher mission as set forth by the army health system in support of our greatest asset, the soldier."[2]

A medical-surgical nurse may be stationed at a field hospital. He or she starts the day by ordering supplies and equipment. Then the medical-surgical nurse supervises equipment maintenance and storage and distribution of supplies. The medical-surgical nurse also supervises a nursing staff, makes schedules to ensure adequate nursing care is available at all times, and coordinates patient admissions and discharges. Medical-surgical nurses help patients needing all types of

★ Part of an army nurse's job is to update patients' medical and surgical records.

care, from tending to soldiers' stomachaches to stitching up severe injuries.

When combat casualties arrive, the nursing staff members have to be ready. They are the first line of triage, working under highly stressful conditions. They keep conditions sterile in the dust and dirt surrounding field facilities. They are prepared for intermittent power outages. They spend hours assisting doctors in surgery. The medical-surgical nurse also arranges transfers to other facilities for patients who need immediate advanced care.

During a shift, the MOS 66H nurse keeps the unit organized, efficient, and on task. The medical-surgical nurse makes quick decisions about who needs care first, supervises other staff members to ensure all patients are receiving proper attention, and makes sure necessary supplies are available and equipment is properly used.

MAKING AN IMPACT

Nurses have been a vital part of the US Army since the Revolutionary War. They have kept soldiers healthy, reduced casualties by providing proper and timely care, and offered moral support in times of crises. The army nurse is a vital line of support for soldiers who need care in the field. However, today's army nurses do not only care for soldiers in the field. They also help veterans and their families adjust to changing circumstances as soldiers move from the army to civilian life. On a personal level, Nurse Corps Officer First Lieutenant Maureen Bickett says of being an army nurse, "I was given traits, leadership abilities and skills that I wouldn't have had if I had just graduated with a regular nursing degree."[6]

SKILLS AND TRAINING

Medical-surgical nurses must be able to concentrate and think critically under stress. The job requires accurate and immediate decision-making that may mean life or death for patients. Medical-surgical nurses must respect both the people they care for and those under their command. They must work with fellow officers. As a leader of a nursing unit, the medical-surgical nurse must have organizational skills and the ability to train others.

This MOS is open at the officer level. Candidates for active duty MOS 66H must have a bachelor's degree as a registered nurse (RN) and a current state nursing license. At least one year of experience working in public health is helpful. A medical-surgical nurse candidate must be a US citizen between 21 and 42 years old. Army Nurse Corps officers do not attend boot camp, but they must complete the Basic Officer Leaders Course (BOLC) to become an army officer. In the BOLC, officers learn about the army health-care system, army doctrine, and soldier and leadership roles. Officers must meet weight, height, and physical fitness standards.

For MOS 66H army reserve, candidates must have, in addition to the above criteria, permanent US residency. Army reserve candidates, who typically work on US army posts, may request a waiver of the age requirements for active soldiers, who are often deployed to other countries.

★ An army health-care specialist, *right*, checks a patient while a
medical-surgical nurse, *left*, records the information into patient records.

Army doctors and nurses need college degrees, but the army also has opportunities in the medical field for people who prefer not to attend college. For example, the combat medic specialist (MOS 68W) specializes in emergency medical treatment in combat. This job requires 16 weeks of advanced training after basic training.

Army medical care isn't limited to humans. Animal care specialists (MOS 68T) are responsible for caring for government-owned animals and preventing the spread of disease from animals to people. MOS 68T soldiers assist army veterinarians in caring for animals. They give oral medications, assist in surgery, care for wounds, and ensure sanitary conditions. MOS 68T candidates need a high school diploma, including one year each of biology and algebra.

TOP FIVE QUESTIONS

★ **CAN A NURSING STUDENT IN COLLEGE JOIN ROTC?**

Yes. The ROTC has a Nurse Training and Scholarship Program that offers two-, three-, and four-year scholarships.

★ **WILL THE ARMY PAY FOR NURSING SCHOOL?**

Yes. Nurses can receive a monthly check from the military while they attend nursing school and are eligible for school loan repayment programs. They receive bonuses when they graduate. Nurses who receive this funding must commit to serving in the reserves or as active duty nurses after graduation.

★ **CAN A PERSON BE AN ARMY NURSE WITH A TWO-YEAR DEGREE?**

No. US Army nurses, like all commissioned officers, must have a four-year bachelor's degree.

★ **HOW CAN BEING AN ARMY NURSE HELP A PERSON'S NURSING CAREER?**

The army teaches leadership and organizational skills that are useful for leadership roles in civilian nursing jobs, such as nursing department heads and hospital administrators.

★ **CAN EXPERIENCE AS AN ARMY NURSE HELP SOMEONE GET A CIVILIAN JOB?**

Several employers, including the prestigious Johns Hopkins Hospital, participate in the Army PaYS program. This program is a cooperative effort between the army and private businesses to guarantee interviews in the civilian world to trained veterans.

CHAPTER 8

MULTIMEDIA ILLUSTRATOR

The US Army produces a lot of educational, promotional and informational materials. Multimedia illustrators (MOS 25M) design recruiting posters, pamphlets, websites, technical illustrations for manuals, unit insignia, and any other product that requires creative and professional graphic design. They create

An army multimedia illustrator works on a large sign, one of the many types of graphics he can design.

reports containing battlefield schematics and graphs. In addition to paper and online products, they also help create training films and even animated cartoons. MOS 25M is part of the Signal Corps, the part of the army charged with communications to support the troops.

During training, people in MOS 25M learn art basics such as design, use of color, and lettering. They learn to use and maintain printers, edit and manipulate images, and use graphics software. Entry-level multimedia illustrators (25M10) operate equipment to create visual presentations and graphs and maintain various multimedia equipment. MOS 25M20 determines what style of graphics will be used, which media are most appropriate, and what the requirements are for production. The 25M30 grade supervises multimedia illustrators and plans, organizes, and assigns new projects.

As an MOS 25M, a soldier may work in the field or on an army post to support a mission. Soldiers in the field often work many hours per day. After physical training and breakfast, an illustrator checks the computers, printers, and other equipment and performs any maintenance needed. As conditions on the

SIGNAL CORPS LEADS THE WAY

The US Army was the world's first army to establish a separate branch for communications, the Signal Corps. The Signal Corps was proposed by General Albert James Myer, using a system called Wigwag. Wigwag, adopted in 1860, was a communication system that used flags and torches. The army used Wigwag during the Civil War, but the telegraph replaced it after the war. In 1870, Congress created the Weather Bureau under the Signal Corps. Myer helped build the National Weather Service, which moved to the Department of Agriculture in 1891. In 1907, the Signal Corps created the aeronautical division to gather information. The Signal Corps hired Wilbur and Orville Wright the next year to test its first airplane. The Wright brothers had made the world's first successful airplane flight in 1903. In 1918, this unit became the Army Air Service, an early version of what is now the US Air Force. By World War I, the Signal Corps used radio telephones, and it had developed radar by World War II. In 1958, it launched its first communications satellite.

★ Some army personnel who work with graphics spend a lot of time at computers.

battlefield change, the illustrator sketches new field positions and other information important to decision-making.

Illustrators use freehand or technical drawing to produce combat graphics used with map overlays. They access data to prepare charts and drawings, which may include information from battlefield reports, satellite images, base maps, and photographs. All available information must be displayed so that commanders have accurate information to review and give to superiors and those in the field.

Other graphic artists create products for psychological warfare or propaganda. Psychological warfare or psychological operations (PSYOPS) involves influencing the morale of civilians in areas of conflict or enemy troops during times of war. Multimedia illustrators work with PSYOPS soldiers to create posters, pamphlets, or other handouts to convince the enemy of the US Army's overwhelming power.

"I WANT YOU"

The most famous US Army poster ever made is probably the "I Want You" poster created in 1917 as a recruiting tool. It showed an image of Uncle Sam with his finger pointing toward the viewer. James Montgomery Flagg (1877–1960) created the poster. Flagg was a well-known graphic artist who created 46 posters between 1917 and 1919 for the US government. The government distributed four million copies of the "I Want You" poster during World War I. The poster was used again for recruiting in World War II. The poster has been recreated over and over by various groups and artists, with some versions including modern political figures.

These graphic products might include flyers encouraging enemy combatants to surrender and the steps in that process.

Propaganda encourages cooperation by using friendly messages. The target audience may be groups, individuals, or even governments. Propaganda may include handouts for civilians that encourage cooperation with US soldiers; posters or videos showing the US Army in a favorable light as an ally; and websites for recruiting.

SKILLS AND TRAINING

This army MOS requires an interest in art, lettering, or visual presentation. Candidates must have a creative eye for graphics

MAKING AN IMPACT

Communication is essential for the army. Whether it's producing accurate, on-time products for battlefield planning or materials that impact the health and welfare of soldiers, multimedia illustrators provide essential information to all levels of soldiers in and out of the field. Multimedia illustrators are an important line of communication between the civilian world and the army. They provide information for recruitment and graphics for distribution to the media, and they create materials to educate the public in how military tax dollars are spent. Private Anthony Torres works as a graphic illustrator. He explains how using his art skills to create army graphics is important. "You'll see a lot of pamphlets, different kinds of posters, unit patches—art that can really impact you by the way you see it," he says.[1]

and color. They should be able to create ideas for visual products, have an eye for detail, and work neatly. Normal color vision is required. An MOS 25M must be a US citizen and pass a secret security clearance because he or she may be required to work with sensitive information in preparing reports and other visuals.

AMERICA'S ARMY: THE GAME

The US Army is always looking for new and innovative recruitment tools. In 1999, Colonel Casey Wardynski developed the idea of *America's Army*, a video game for teens. Released in 2002, the first-person shooter game allows players to explore roles in the army and teaches the army's core seven values: loyalty, duty, respect, selfless service, honor, integrity, and personal courage. New games in the official series include *America's Army: Proving Grounds* and *America's Army: True Soldiers*. In addition to the video games, people can also learn about soldiers' lives in online comic books called the *America's Army Comics*.

This MOS is open to both active and reserve soldiers. It requires an ASVAB score of 93 in electronics and a 91 in skilled technical. In addition, candidates should have some background in graphics and multimedia, such as an associate's degree in graphic design or related work experience. Upon enlistment, soldiers have nine weeks of basic combat training, followed by thirteen weeks and one day of Advanced Individual Training. Training is conducted at Fort Meade, Maryland, the location of the US Cyber Command and Defense Information Systems Agency. MOS 25M may get certifications

★ Multimedia illustrators help with all types of graphics and print materials, including military base magazines.

★ A US Army soldier films video in Baghdad, Iraq, in 2007.

in Illustrator, Photoshop, Dreamweaver, or many other graphic software programs.

Another MOS closely related to multimedia illustrator is the MOS 25V, combat documentation/production specialist. These soldiers use still photographs and video equipment to document other soldiers during military operations. They may be deployed to combat zones to photograph battlefield conditions or they may be soldiers working with civilian populations. They must be ready for anything. As Sergeant Ambraea Johnson says, "You have to come ready to learn at all times. Technology is constantly changing."[2]

TOP FIVE QUESTIONS

★ **DOES SOMEONE HAVE TO BE A GREAT ARTIST TO BE AN MOS 25M?**

Enlistees should have experience in freehand drawing and computer illustration. They must work neatly and creatively to design products.

★ **DO PEOPLE WHO WANT TO WORK AS MOS 25M GET ANY CREDIT FOR SKILLS AND EXPERIENCE GAINED BEFORE THEY JOINED THE ARMY?**

This MOS is available for the Army Civilian Acquired Skills Program, which gives recruits the chance of an accelerated promotion to specialist if they have skills acquired as civilians. Enlistees in MOS 25M can get credit for a relevant associate degree in a vocational or technical school, a bachelor's degree in graphic design, or two years of training and/or experience in graphics design, photo manipulation, multimedia presentations, and electronic page layout.

★ **IS THIS MOS OPEN TO MEMBERS OF THE NATIONAL GUARD?**

Yes. This MOS is available to active duty soldiers, National Guard, and reserves.

★ **DO SOLDIERS HAVE TO BE IN GREAT PHYSICAL SHAPE FOR THIS MOS?**

All soldiers are required to be in good physical shape. MOS 25M is rated moderately heavy in its physical requirements. Soldiers are expected to move and set up heavy equipment such as copy machines in the field.

★ **WHAT OTHER JOBS ARE AVAILABLE IN THE SIGNAL CORPS?**

The Signal Corps uses a wide range of technologies for communication and data collection. The Signal Corps currently has 16 MOS, each specializing in areas of communication ranging from cable installation (25L) to using cameras, video, and audio equipment for documenting combat in the field (25V).

CHAPTER 9

CULINARY SPECIALIST

The culinary specialist (MOS 92G) is responsible for preparing and serving food as well as maintaining and operating kitchen equipment for army soldiers. Entry-level positions involve preparing food, such as peeling potatoes or chopping vegetables. These soldiers do basic cooking with army recipes and set up serving lines. After meals, they clean and take down field kitchens.

Army culinary specialists often need to set up field kitchens outside. They cook and serve food in these small kitchens.

More experienced soldiers supervise the work and are responsible for food safety. They make sure that proper procedures are used for cooking and storing food. Their understanding of chemical reactions involved in cooking and food spoilage helps keep food safe. Culinary specialists are responsible for ordering food items, food service accounting, and cooking more difficult menus. At higher levels, culinary specialists prepare menus, making sure that meals meet the calorie and nutritional needs of soldiers. They may oversee military contractors, which are civilians or nonmilitary businesses providing services to the army.

Feeding up to 800 soldiers three meals a day from a field kitchen is not an easy task.[1] Field kitchen workers learn how to use and maintain equipment specifically designed to quickly feed large numbers of people in a small space. Culinary specialists must have good time management skills and work as a team to get the job done. The field kitchens are often hot, and it takes strength to handle much of the large equipment.

MREs

Soldiers can't always make it to a field station for meals. Soldiers who expect to spend a long time in the field take Meals Ready to Eat (MREs). MREs are sealed foil pouches. The pouches have an entrée such as spaghetti or beef stew; a side dish such as rice or fruit; crackers with peanut butter, jelly, or cheese spread; a cookie or cake for dessert; cocoa or another beverage which can be added to water; candy; condiments; and utensils. Although the MREs can be eaten cold, they come with a flameless heater to warm the entrée. MREs come with a choice of 24 entrées. Each MRE provides approximately 1,250 calories. MREs must be able to survive a 1,250-foot (381 m) parachute drop or 100-foot (30 m) straight drop. They will last 3.5 years at 80 degrees (27°C) or nine months at 100 degrees (38°C).

BUSY DAYS

Culinary specialists expect days filled with many hours of hard work. They are in the kitchen early preparing breakfast so the food is ready when the other soldiers arrive. They set up for service, making sure the food looks as good as it tastes. After serving, they clean up and start preparation for the midday meal. This means carrying heavy boxes of supplies, properly storing them, and preparing meats and other foods. They bake and garnish desserts. They make sure there is an adequate supply of filtered water and that all the food they need is on hand.

The midday meal is followed by another cleanup. The workers then store leftovers that may be used later and begin getting ready for the evening meal. In field kitchen situations, conditions are often hot and dusty. Culinary specialists want to ensure that when a soldier sits down to eat, it is a pleasant experience. Sergeant Monique Sorrell says, "The quality of food you provide your soldiers is going to boost their morale and keep them happy doing their jobs."[2]

MAKING AN IMPACT

Food is vital to an army's strength and morale. The job of supplying three nutritious and satisfying meals a day to thousands of soldiers is essential. It takes a massive effort to make sure food supplies are safe, organized, and ready to eat when soldiers arrive for their meal. The culinary specialists that make this happen are a well-trained, efficient, and caring group of people. Private First Class Judy Luna explains, "Most rewarding is when you see their faces come in and they see *food*. Not only do they see food, they see good nutritious food."[3]

US ARMY CULINARY ARTS TEAM

Army culinary specialists have opportunities for special training as pastry chefs and master chefs. The Department of Defense and the American Culinary Federation (ACF), a civilian organization of 17,000 chefs, have partnered for more than 40 years to train military chefs and provide better food for military personnel. The ACF supports a yearly competition, the Joint Culinary Training Exercise, for chefs from across the military, including the US Army Culinary Arts Team. Soldiers who are awarded medals from the competition also receive credits toward ACF certification, which can help toward army promotion. Additionally, the skills gained from this competition can help army culinary specialists get food service jobs after they leave the army.

Once everyone has eaten the three meals of the day, the culinary specialists still have to clean up again and prepare for the next day. They may check for special dietary needs and review menus. Equipment also has to be cleaned and maintained for the next day. In larger units, cooks may work shifts. This may be one shift from 4:00 a.m. to noon and another from noon to 8:00 p.m.

SKILLS AND TRAINING

Soldiers working in MOS 92G must have an interest in food and cooking as well as in health and nutrition. They should have an aptitude for accounting, math, and chemistry. Candidates must have an ASVAB score of 85 in operators and food, and they must have normal color vision.

★ Soldiers unpack a box of food supplies.

MOS 92G requires ten weeks of basic combat training, followed by nine weeks of Advanced Individual Training with on-the-job instruction. During training, soldiers learn how to prepare standard army menus and menus for special dietary needs. They learn how to order food and kitchen supplies and how to properly store perishable foods.

MANY OPPORTUNITIES

MOS 92G is just one job available to soldiers, as the army has many career paths. More than 150 jobs are available for soldiers in the US Army. They are in areas including art, medicine, computers, mechanics, cooking, and combat. The Department of Defense is the nation's largest employer, with more than three million employees.[4]

Enlisting in the US Army provides training that is often applicable to jobs in the civilian world. There are also long-term army careers that provide many benefits including insurance and retirement. An army enlistee's career choice depends on his or her interests and aptitudes. Specialist Gagan Dhiman (MOS 91B, wheeled vehicle mechanic) says, "If you want to succeed and you have a passion for anything at all, the opportunity is endless."[5]

★ TOP FIVE QUESTIONS

★ HOW CAN SKILLS THAT A PERSON HAS BEFORE ENLISTING IN THE ARMY BE APPLIED TO MOS 92G?

MOS 92G is part of the Army Civilian Acquired Skills Program. Enlistees with two years of formal training and/or experience in food preparation in commercial or institutional settings may apply to start at a higher rank. However, working in fast-food preparation doesn't count in the program.

★ CAN PEOPLE GET FINANCIAL BONUSES FOR ENLISTING AS CULINARY SPECIALISTS?

At times, the army finds it hard to fill certain jobs, so it offers enlistment bonuses, or money paid up front to enlistees, to attract more people to these jobs. Culinary specialists have earned up to a $7,000 enlistment bonus. Check online to see which MOS the army is offering bonuses for.

★ HOW MANY PEOPLE DO ARMY CULINARY SPECIALISTS COOK FOR?

Culinary specialists can expect to cook and serve for as few as 25 people and up to 1,300 people per meal.

★ CAN A PERSON DO THIS JOB IN THE NATIONAL GUARD?

Yes. MOS 92G is open to active duty soldiers, reserves, and the National Guard.

★ WHAT CIVILIAN CAREERS WILL THIS JOB PREPARE PEOPLE FOR?

Culinary specialists may find jobs working in many food preparation places, including restaurants, schools, hotels, hospitals, or corporations with their own food service facilities. This MOS is part of the PaYS program that guarantees an interview with a participating corporation for a civilian job after army service.

ESSENTIAL FACTS

★ ★

US ARMY HISTORY

★ 1775: The Second Continental Congress forms the Continental army.

★ 1802: The US Military Academy opens in West Point, New York.

★ 1899: US Secretary of War Elihu Root begins reorganization of the army.

★ 1917: The United States enters World War I, and the US Army drafts soldiers.

★ 1941: The United States enters World War II, and the army expands, eventually reaching 8.3 million troops.

★ 1947: The US Department of War becomes the Department of Defense.

★ 1973: The draft ends and the army becomes an all-volunteer force.

★ 1991: The army uses new high-tech equipment during the Persian Gulf War.

★ 2010: US Army Cyber Command is established.

★ 2014: Army combat missions related to the War on Terror officially end in Afghanistan.

US ARMY ORGANIZATION

The US Army is organized in a hierarchical fashion. The army chief of staff, the highest military position in the army, reports to the civilian leadership of the US military, the secretary of defense, and the president. Individual soldiers have a hierarchy of ranks. Enlisted ranks begin at private and end with sergeant. The higher enlisted ranks, corporal and sergeant, are called noncommissioned officers. Above noncommissioned officers are warrant officers, who are technical specialists. Commissioned officers are the upper ranks of the army, beginning with lieutenant and moving up through captain, major, colonel, and general. As soldiers move up the ranks, they are assigned to units of increasing size and more responsibility.

CAREER MOVES

How can you prepare for a career in the US Army?

★ Take relevant classes in high school such as math and science.

★ Explore the options available for jobs on the US Army websites.

★ Get experience in your field of interest by taking extra classes or getting a job that would provide relevant work experience.

★ Explore options for college tuition through the army.

★ Talk to parents or friends who have army experience.

★ Talk to an army recruiter about your interests and options.

IMPACT ON SOCIETY

From the Revolutionary War to today, the US Army has kept the United States safe from enemies. It plays a vital role in maintaining democracy and protecting allies of our country around the world. It is also at the forefront of technological innovation for military and civilian use. Army service can help young people transition into adults by teaching them responsibility and self-discipline. It pushes people to be the best they can be. Joining the US Army is also a way to further education, which benefits the individual and society as a whole. Service in the US Army makes a person a part of a community of Americans that take pride in defending their country.

QUOTE

"Army strong, to me, meant that if you were good, you were going to be the best."

—Major Otto Padron, an army reserve infantry officer

GLOSSARY

amphibious
Working in both land and water.

aptitude
A natural ability to do something or learn something.

cadet
A student or trainee in the armed services.

civilian
A person not serving in the armed forces.

draft
A system in which people of a certain age are required to register for military service.

drill
Training in military movements and use of weapons.

enlist
To voluntarily join the military.

Homeland Security
The US government's efforts and strategies aimed at protecting the United States.

infrared imaging
Imaging used to detect items not seen in visible light.

insurgent
A person who fights against a government or other authority.

integration
Acceptance of people belonging to different groups (such as races) as equals in society.

intelligence
Information that is of military or political value.

marksmanship
The skill of shooting at and hitting a target.

militia
A military force made up of nonprofessional fighters.

mortar
A front-loaded cannon used to fire shells in a high arc.

pay grade
Base pay determined by rank and length of military service.

radar
A technology that involves bouncing radio waves off of distant objects to determine their location, size, and speed.

rank
An individual's position in military hierarchy.

segregated
Separated based on race, gender, ethnicity, or other factors.

triangulation
The process of using the distance to three objects to pinpoint a location.

veteran
A person who previously served in the military.

ADDITIONAL RESOURCES

Selected Bibliography

"The Army History Center." *US Army Historical Foundation*, n.d., armyhistory.org. Accessed 18 Sept. 2019.

"Careers and Jobs." *US Army*, n.d., goarmy.com. Accessed 18 Sept. 2019.

"The History and Roles of the U.S. Army." *Military.com*, 2019, military.com. Accessed 18 Sept. 2019.

Further Readings

Brandus, Paul. *This Day in U.S. Military History*. Bernan, 2020.

Lusted, Marcia Amidon. *US Special Operations Forces*. Abdo, 2021.

Uschan, Michael V. *Careers in the US Army*. ReferencePoint Press, 2016.

Online Resources

To learn more about the US Army, please visit **abdobooklinks.com** or scan this QR code. These links are routinely monitored and updated to provide the most current information available.

More Information

For more information on this subject, contact or visit the following organizations:

US Army Heritage and Education Center
950 Soldiers Dr.
Carlisle, PA 17013
717-245-3972
ahec.armywarcollege.edu

Part of the historic US Army War College, the US Army Heritage and Education Center offers exhibits that are open to the public, providing information about the army's history and legacy.

US Army Historical Foundation
2425 Wilson Blvd.
Arlington, VA 22201
800-506-2672
armyhistory.org

The nonprofit Army Historical Foundation works to preserve the history and heritage of the US Army through publications, research, and educational programs.

SOURCE NOTES

CHAPTER 1. CLEARING THE WAY

1. Tayja Kuligowski. "48 Interesting U.S. Military Facts." *Fact Retriever*, 15 Oct. 2017, factretriever.com. Accessed 16 Dec. 2019.

2. Dawn Rosenberg McKay. "Best Army Jobs: Highest Paying Jobs in the U.S. Army." *Balance Careers*, 25 June 2019, thebalancecareers.com. Accessed 16 Dec. 2019.

3. Donovan Slack, John Kelly, and James Sergent. "Death Rates, Bedsores, ER Wait Times: Where Every VA Hospital Lags or Leads Other Medical Care." *USA Today*, 7 Feb. 2019, usatoday.com. Accessed 16 Dec. 2019.

CHAPTER 2. THE HISTORY OF THE US ARMY

1. "Buffalo Soldier." *Encyclopedia Britannica*, 20 Aug. 2019, britannica.com. Accessed 16 Dec. 2019.

2. "The United States Army." *Encyclopedia Britannica*, 12 Dec. 2019, britannica.com. Accessed 16 Dec. 2019.

3. "The United States Army."

4. "History Explorer: The Nisei Soldiers." *National Museum of American History*, 30 June 2014, americanhistory.si.edu. Accessed 16 Dec. 2019.

5. "The United States Army."

6. "The United States Army."

7. "Persian Gulf War." *Encyclopedia Britannica*, 7 Mar. 2019, britannica.com. Accessed 16 Dec. 2019.

8. "September 11 Terror Attacks Fast Facts." *CNN*, 13 Nov. 2019, cnn.com. Accessed 16 Dec. 2019.

9. "What Is the Army?" *US Army*, 10 July 2018, goarmy.com. Accessed 16 Dec. 2019.

CHAPTER 3. THE US ARMY TODAY

1. "Military Reserve Drill Pay Chart for 2020." *Military Rates*, 2019, militaryrates.com. Accessed 16 Dec. 2019.

2. "Climbing the Corporate Ladder Thanks to the U.S. Army." *US Army*, 23 Aug. 2017, goarmy.com. Accessed 16 Dec. 2019.

3. "History." *Women in the Army*, n.d., army.mil. Accessed 16 Dec. 2019.

4. Rod Powers. "How the U.S. Army is Organized." *Balance Careers*, 26 Apr. 2019, thebalancecareers.com. Accessed 16 Dec. 2019.

CHAPTER 4. INFANTRY

1. Stewart Smith. "What Does an Infantryman (11B) Do?: Learn about the Salary, Required Skills, & More." *Balance Careers*, 25 June 2019, thebalancecareers.com. Accessed 16 Dec. 2019.

2. "What Do Soldiers Carry and What Does It Weigh?" *PTX*, n.d., ptxnomad.com. Accessed 16 Dec. 2019.

3. "Training Soldiers to Be Their Best." *US Army*, 23 Aug. 2017, goarmy.com. Accessed 16 Dec. 2019.

CHAPTER 5. GEOSPATIAL INTELLIGENCE IMAGERY ANALYST

1. "Army MOS 35G Geospatial Intelligence Imagery Analyst." *YouTube*, uploaded by Army Kansas City Recruiting Battalion, 1 Apr. 2019, youtube.com. Accessed 16 Dec. 2019.

CHAPTER 6. CONSTRUCTION EQUIPMENT REPAIRER

1. Dawn Arden. "91L Course, Teaching Skills that Reach Beyond the Military." *Guidon*, 3 May 2018, myguidon.com. Accessed 16 Dec. 2019.

SOURCE NOTES CONTINUED

CHAPTER 7. MEDICAL-SURGICAL NURSE

1. "Dr. Anita Newcomb McGee." *Changing the Face of Medicine*, 3 June 2015, cfmedicine.nlm.nih.gov. Accessed 16 Dec. 2019.

2. John Moore. "Call to Service: A Transition from Civilian to Army Nurse." *US Army*, 6 May 2019, army.mil. Accessed 16 Dec. 2019.

3. "The Evolution of Male Army Nurse Corps." *US Army Medical Department*, 7 July 2009, history.amedd.army.mil. Accessed 16 Dec. 2019.

4. Jennifer Larson. "12 Interesting Facts about Military Nurses." *Travel Nursing*, 2015, travelnursing.com. Accessed 16 Dec. 2019.

5. David Auerbach, Peter Buerhaus, Douglas Staiger, and Lucy Skinner. "2017 Data Brief Update: Current Trends of Men in Nursing." *Montana State University*, 8 Apr. 2017, healthworkforcestudies.com. Accessed 16 Dec. 2019.

6. "How ROTC Gave One Army Nurse the Self-Discipline to Support Soldiers and a Family." *US Army*, 18 May 2017, goarmy.com. Accessed 16 Dec. 2019.

CHAPTER 8. MULTIMEDIA ILLUSTRATOR

1. "Graphic Illustrator ARMY Feature." *YouTube*, uploaded by Joseph Aleman, 25 Nov 2018, youtube.com. Accessed 16 Dec. 2019.

2. "25V MOS: What to Expect During a Deployment." *YouTube*, uploaded by The Official Rickey Bowden, 13 Nov. 2018, youtube.com. Accessed 16 Dec. 2019.

CHAPTER 9. CULINARY SPECIALIST

1. "Army Field Feeding Systems." *US Army*, n.d., quartermaster.army.mil. Accessed 16 Dec. 2019.

2. "Being a 92G – Food Service Specialist in the Army." *YouTube*, uploaded by GOARMY.COM, 18 May 2012, youtube.com. Accessed 16 Dec. 2019.

3. "92G - Culinary Specialist." *YouTube*, uploaded by CASCOM Public Affairs, 6 July 2016, youtube.com. Accessed 16 Dec. 2019.

4. Tayja Kuligowski. "48 Interesting U.S. Military Facts." *Fact Retriever*, 15 Oct. 2017, factretriever.com. Accessed 16 Dec. 2019.

5. "Part Photographer, Part Mechanic, All Army Reserve." *US Army*, 1 May 2017, goarmy.com. Accessed 16 Dec. 2019.

INDEX

ABOUT THE AUTHOR

Cynthia Kennedy Henzel

Cynthia Kennedy Henzel has a bachelor's degree in social studies education and a master's in geography. She has worked as a teacher-educator in many countries. Currently, she works writing fiction and nonfiction books and developing education materials for social studies, history, science, and English language learner students. She has written more than 85 books and 150 stories for young people.